PARTY GAMES

The Diagram Group

BROCKHAMPTON
DIAGRAM
GUIDES

Party Games

© Diagram Visual Information Ltd. 1997
  195 Kentish Town Road
  London
  NW5 2JU

First published in Great Britain in 1997 by
Brockhampton Press Ltd
20 Bloomsbury Street
London
WC1 2QA
a member of the Hodder Headline Group PLC

ISBN 1-86019-744-2

Also in this series:
Calligraphy
Card Games
How the Body Works
Identifying Architecture
Kings and Queens of Britain
Magic Tricks
Soccer Skills

Introduction

The games described in this book can be relied upon to liven up all kinds of parties. Old favourites have been brought together with games you might never have encountered before. Suitable for ages 5 and upwards, most of these games will take between 5 and 15 minutes to play. For each one there is a list of what you will need, step-by-step instructions for play and a clear statement of the winning conditions. Once you have grasped the general principles of each game, try making up your own variations to suit different situations.

Contents

RATTLESNAKES!

This is a game for any number of players aged 5–10 years. It lasts 5–15 minutes.

You will need

Two blindfolds, two empty tins and some coins. Make sure there are no sharp edges on the tins.

Playing

Two volunteers are chosen to be the 'rattlesnakes'. They are blindfolded and everyone else surrounds them in a circle. Each rattlesnake is led to an opposite side of the circle and given a tin to hold. The tin contains a few coins so that it rattles loudly when shaken. The host spins each snake around a few times and then shouts 'GO!' The snakes have to try and find each other, but both must remain within the circle. To help them locate each other the snakes may shake their tins (or 'rattles') – when one snake rattles the other must do so as well.

Winning

The winner is the first snake to touch the other. When this happens two more 'rattlesnakes' are selected and another round is played.

HAT PARADE

This is a game for any number of players aged 10 and over and lasts about 10–15 minutes.

You will need
Several pairs of scissors, crayons, some large sheets of paper and some sticky tape.

Playing
Each player is given a few sheets of paper and, if possible, a pair of scissors each. Everyone should also have crayons and sticky tape. The aim of this game is to make the best hat you can within a certain time period, say ten or fifteen minutes. When time is up, players have to wear their hats in a 'hat parade'.

Winning
The player who has created the most attractive or amusing hat is the winner.

BEETLE

This is a game for any number of players aged 5–10 years. It lasts about 5–15 minutes.

You will need

Each player needs some paper and a pencil. You will also need a single die.

Playing

Each player takes a turn at throwing the die. Each of the numbers on the die corresponds to a part of the beetle. A player may draw only that part of the beetle which corresponds to the number they have thrown. Players must throw a 'one' (the body) to start, and cannot draw the feelers or eyes until they have thrown a 'two' and drawn the head. Players must throw 'three', 'four' and 'five' *twice*, as each beetle has two legs, two eyes and two antennae.

Winning

The winner is the first player to draw a complete beetle.

Beetle body parts
1 Body
2 Head
3 One leg
4 One eye
5 One antenna
6 Tail

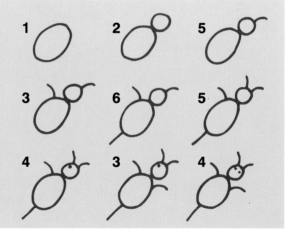

HUMAN ALPHABET

This is a game for 4 or more players aged 10 or over. It usually lasts a minimum of 15 minutes.

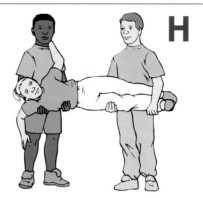

Playing

Divide everybody into equal teams of at least three players. Teams then attempt to make letters of the alphabet using only their own bodies. They may stand up, lean on each other, lie down or hold each other. Teams are awarded a point for the best-formed letter.

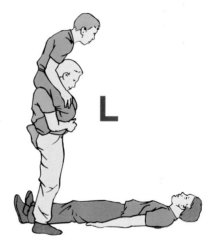

Winning

When all 26 letters have been attempted, points are totalled up and the team with the most wins.

WHO AM I?

This is a game for 2–10 players aged 10 or over. It lasts a minimum of 15 minutes.

You will need

Blank postcards, pencils and sticky tape. Before the game print the names of famous personalities on the cards. You will need about four name-cards per player.

Playing

Decide how long the game will last – 15 minutes to half an hour is best. Each person has a name-card stuck to their back, but they are not allowed to read what is on it. Cards bearing female names can be stuck on the back of male players and cards bearing male names on the back of female players. Everybody then has to walk around the room and ask questions of each other to try and find clues to their new 'identity'. Questions may only be answered 'yes' or 'no'. When a player thinks she has worked out her secret identity she may make a guess, and receives a point if she is right. She then receives a new name-card and returns to the game.

Am I under 30? – NO
Am I British? – NO
Am I American? – YES
Am I a politician? – NO
Am I an entertainer? – YES
Am I a singer? – YES
Am I Madonna? – NO
Am I Diana Ross? – YES!

Winning

The winner is the player who has scored the most points at the end of the agreed time.

BALLOON RACE

This is a game for 2–10 players aged 5 or over. It lasts a minimum of 5 minutes.

You will need
Two inflated balloons.

Playing
The guests are separated into two teams of equal numbers. Each team forms a line, side by side. A balloon is given to the team member at the front of each line. On the word 'GO!' they pass the balloon backwards over their heads to the players behind them in the line. Each player down the line takes the balloon from the person in front of them, and passes it over their head to the person behind them. As soon as the person at the end of the line gets the balloon she runs to the front of the line and passes it between her legs to the person behind. This continues until the player who started at the front of the line is back in that position.

Winning
The winning team is the team which is first to reach its original position. If a team bursts its balloon, the other team automatically wins.

DOWN THE LINE

This is a game for 10–15 players aged 5–10 years. It lasts a minimum of 5 minutes.

You will need
Two chairs and about 24 ordinary, small items such as matchboxes, spoons, vegetables, pencils, etc.

Playing
Divide the players into two teams of equal numbers. Spread the teams out into two rows, spaced as far apart from each other as the room allows. Place a chair next to the first player in each line, and on the chair place twelve items. It does not matter if there are different items on

each chair. On the word 'GO!', the first player in each team picks up an item and passes it to the player behind. The item is passed down the line from player to player, until it reaches the end player who passes it back along to the front again. Meanwhile, the player at the front must concentrate on passing all of the other items to the player behind him, one at a time. When the player at the front receives an item back he must place it on the chair and not touch it again.

Winning

The winning team is the first to pass all twelve items down the line and back again. Every object must complete the journey from one end of the line to the other and back again.

BATTLESHIPS!

This is a game for 2–10 players aged 10 or over and lasts 10–20 minutes.

You will need

Paper and pencils for each player.

Preparation

Guests team up into pairs and each pair draws two grids (see the example opposite) on separate sheets of paper. Label the grids A to J horizontally, and 1 to 10, vertically so that any square in the grids can be referred to by its letter-number coordinates. Each player then draws in his fleet of ships on his home-grid. This information should be kept secret.

Each player's fleet comprises:

a One battleship (four squares in a straight line either horizontal or vertical).
b Two cruisers (three squares in a straight line either horizontal or vertical).
c Three destroyers (two squares in a line either horizontal or vertical).
d Four submarines (one square).

There must be at least one blank square between each ship.

Playing

Each player takes a turn at calling out a grid reference (e.g. B3) to their opponent, who must answer 'hit', if that square on his home-grid contains part of a ship, or 'miss', if it does not. Players aim to 'hit' every enemy square that contains a ship. Players should mark every square they choose on their enemy-grid to keep track of where they have already fired shots. Players must answer 'hit' if their opponent correctly guesses the location of one of their ships, then draw a mark through it on their home-grid to show that the square has been hit. A ship is sunk when all of the squares it covers have been hit.

Winning
The winner is the first player to sink all of their opponent's ships.

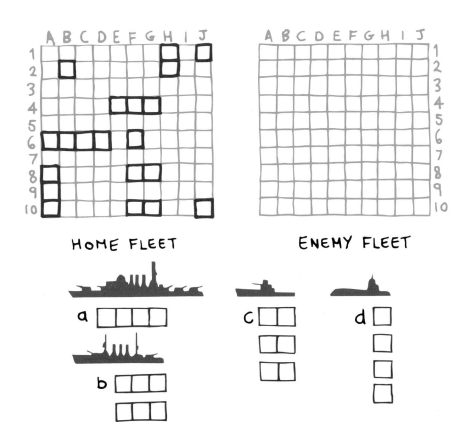

HOME FLEET   ENEMY FLEET

RICE PICKERS

This is a game for any number of players aged 10 or older. It lasts between 5–15 minutes.

You will need
Two bowls, one of which contains a small amount of uncooked rice, and two chopsticks (or you could use knitting needles).

Playing
Place the bowls side by side on the floor or on a table. Each player in turn has a set time (say 30 seconds) to transfer as many grains of rice as possible to the empty bowl, using only the chopsticks. Players are not allowed to touch or move the bowls in any way.

Winning
The player who successfully transfers the most grains of rice to the empty bowl within the set time is the winner.

INTO THE HAT

This is a game for any number of players aged 10 or over. It usually lasts a minimum of 5 minutes.

You will need
Two packs of playing cards with different coloured backs and a hat (or you could use a small bowl).

Preparation
Separate the players into two teams and line them up on opposite sides of the room. Each team nominates a captain who is given a pack of cards. The captains then deal out the pack of cards among their team mates as equally as possible. Place the hat in the middle of the room at an equal distance from each team.

Playing
Each player takes a turn at throwing their cards into the hat. Count up how many cards from each pack are in the hat only after all cards have been thrown.

Winning
Whichever team has the most cards in the hat is the winner for that round. Further rounds are played. The first team to win three rounds wins the game.

NAME THEM!

This is a game for any number of players aged 10 or over. It usually lasts 5–15 minutes.

You will need
Paper and pencils for each player.

Playing
Prepare a list of 15 famous people and write down their first names and surnames in a mixed up list. Players are given a time limit (10 minutes, for example) in which to match the surnames to the first names.

Examples of mixed up famous names

1. Bruno
2. Albert
3. Bob
4. Anne
5. James
6. Dylan
7. Bill
8. Nicholson
9. Davis
10. Einstein
11. Oliver
12. Nightingale
13. Eliot
14. Mary
15. Chaplin
16. Jack
17. Florence
18. Boleyn
19. Cromwell
20. Clinton
21. Cole
22. George
23. Frank
24. Shelley
25. Porter
26. Hardy
27. Charlie
28. Joyce
29. Miles
30. Thomas

Winning
The winner is the player who correctly reconstructs the most names.

HAVEN'T I SEEN YOU SOMEWHERE BEFORE?

This is a game for 2–10 players aged 10 or over. It usually lasts a minimum of 5 minutes.

You will need
A pencil and a piece of paper for each player, some glossy magazines and some thin card or plain paper.

Playing
Tear out ten pictures of faces from the magazines and number them on the back from one to ten. Write ten made-up names (Leon, Susan, Ahmed, etc.) on ten pieces of card and place one under each face. Keep a secret note of which name goes with which face. Let everyone study the names and faces for two minutes and then remove them. After a further minute lay out the names and faces again, but this time, in a different order. Players must write down which name originally went with each face, starting with the face to the far left of the row.

Winning
The winner is the person who correctly matches the most names to their original faces.

SPOT THE CHANGES!

This is a game for any number of players ages 5–10 years. It lasts 5–15 minutes.

You will need
Half-a-dozen household objects and a tablecloth.

Playing
Place some of the objects on a table and then cover them with the cloth. Sit everyone around in a circle then lift the cloth and allow the players to study the objects for one minute. After a minute, cover the objects again and get everyone to turn their backs. Now rearrange the objects in some way; change their position, take one away or replace one with a new object. Once everyone has turned around again remove the cloth and challenge the players to spot the change. Players should write down their guess on a piece of paper without letting anyone else see. Award a point to every player who guesses correctly and then play another round.

Some household objects that could be used in this game

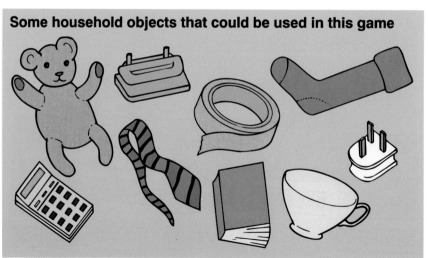

Winning

The winner is the player who has the highest number of points at the end of a given number of rounds.

SHADOW FIGURES

This is a game for any number of players aged 10 or over and lasts about 10–15 minutes.

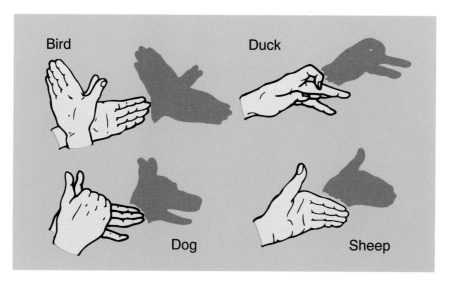

Bird

Duck

Dog

Sheep

You will need
A projector screen (or a white wall or tablecloth) and a strong, directable lamp.

Playing
Each guest is allocated an animal or other subject and shown how to make a shadow-shape of it with their hands. Players are given a few minutes to practise making their shadow-shape and then each player gives a performance to the other guests, using sound effects where necessary!

Winning
This game is played for entertainment only, so there is no winner.

JIGSAW HUNT

This is a game for 2–10 players aged 10 or over and lasts 15–20 minutes.

You will need

Two jigsaws, both about the same size and with not too many pieces. They should be quite different in style so that their pieces can easily be told apart.

Playing

Put together part of the jigsaws and then hide the rest of the pieces all over the house in places where they are not too difficult to find. Guests are divided into two teams and search for the missing pieces from one jigsaw or the other. Once the missing pieces have been found they are put into their correct positions in the jigsaws. Pieces belonging to the opponents' jigsaw must not be moved if found.

Winning

The winning team is the first team to complete their jigsaw. Teams which remove hidden pieces of their opponents' jigsaw are automatically disqualified.

WHEEL OF FORTUNE

This is a game for any number of players aged 10 or over. It lasts 5–15 minutes.

You will need
Cardboard, a large sheet of paper, a pen and a pin (see illustration, *right*).

Preparation
Draw a large circle on the sheet of paper and divide it into sixteen equal segments. In each segment write predictions (fortunes), like those found in newspaper horoscopes. Next, attach the circle to the floor or to a wall, in a position where it can be seen by all players. Cut out the shape of an arrow from your piece of cardboard and pin it to the centre of the sheet so that it will spin round freely.

Playing
Players take it in turn to spin the wheel of fortune and read out their horoscope to the other players.

Winning
There are no winners, this is a game for fun only.

Variation
Some people like to write forfeits instead of fortunes on their wheel. Forfeits might be things like: drinking a glass of water in one go, blowing up several balloons very quickly, being tickled or having to make everyone laugh.

WHICH CURRENCY?

This is a game for 2–10 players aged 10 or over. It lasts 5–15 minutes.

You will need
Paper and pencils for each player.

Preparation
The host is the quizmaster and draws up a list of clues. Here are some examples:

Examples of clues:

1 In which currency would you pay for borscht?
2 In which currency would you pay for a glass of local champagne?
3 In which currency would you pay for a trip on a gondola?
4 In which currency would you pay for a visit to Rembrandt's house?
5 In which currency would you pay for lederhosen?
6 In which currency would you pay for a trip on the blue train?
7 In which currency would you pay for a tour of Jerusalem?

Playing
Players, working either on their own or in small equal teams, write down the answers to each of the questions being asked.

Winning
The winner is the player (or team) with the most correct answers.

PASS IT ON!

This is a game for 2–10 players aged 10 or over. It lasts 5–15 minutes.

You will need
Two fairly large oranges.

Playing
Divide the guests into two equal teams and line them up side by side. Both teams should sit on the floor with their legs stretched out in front of them and their shoes off. Balance an orange on the ankles of the first player in each team. Players have to pass the team's orange along the line using only their ankles. If the orange falls to the floor it is picked up by the host and returned to the first player in the line again.

Winning
The winning team is the first to successfully pass the orange from one end of their line to the other.

HAPPY TRAVELLERS

This is a game for 2–10 players aged 10 or over. It lasts 5–15 minutes.

You will need

Enough copies of identical newspapers to give one to each player.

Preparation

Guests are divided into two teams who sit facing each other in two rows. It is important that players are seated close to each other and that players at each end of the rows have a wall or piece of furniture next to them so that they do not have too much elbow room. Shuffle all the pages in the newspapers and give one to each player. Pages can be upside-down, back-to-front or in the wrong order. It is important to shuffle all newspapers in the same way so that the game is fair.

Playing

On the command 'GO!', all players have to rearrange
their pages so that their newspaper is in the correct order.
This involves a lot of rustling and shoving but players
may not leave their seats or harm the player next to them
in any way; this is a team game so getting in the way of
your neighbour will make it less likely that your team
will win.

Winning

The winning team is the first to sort all their newspapers
into the correct order.

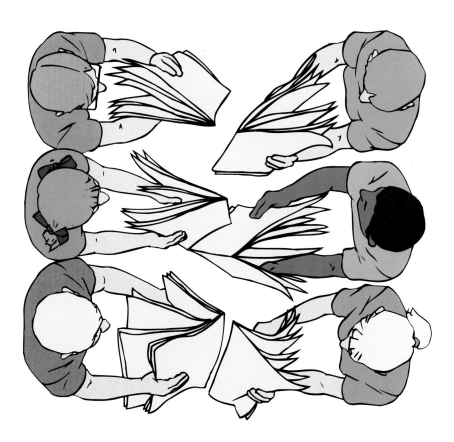

ANKLE GUESSING

This is a game for any number of players aged 10 or over. It lasts 5–15 minutes.

You will need
A large blanket or sheet.

Preparation
Guests are split into two groups (boys and girls, for example). One group leaves the room while the other team members take off their shoes and socks and lie down underneath the blanket. It is important that only their ankles are visible and that no part of their clothing can be seen which might make them easier to identify.

Playing
The first team re-enters the room and has to guess the identities of all those under the blanket from their feet and ankles only. The teams then reverse roles.

Winning
The winner is the player who makes the most correct guesses.

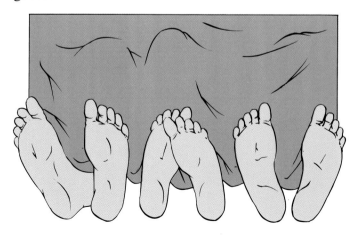

TRADE MARKS

This is a game for 2–10 players aged 10 or over. It lasts 5–15 minutes.

You will need
Enough pencils and paper for each player.

Preparation
Prior to the game, collect about 20 trade marks or logos from advertisements or labels. It is important that these are cut carefully from the name of the product so that only the trademark or logo remains. All the logos should be clearly numbered.

Playing
Each player is challenged to guess the name of each product, identifying it from the logo or trademark alone.

Winning
The player who makes the most correct guesses is the winner.

HUMAN NOUGHTS-AND-CROSSES

This is a game for 10–15 players aged 10 or over. It usually lasts 5–15 minutes. This game cannot be played with less than 10 players.

You will need
Nine strong chairs or a grid marked onto the floor with chalk or ribbon.

Playing
The chairs are placed in three rows of three, each representing a square in a noughts-and-crosses game. This game is played just like noughts-and-crosses on paper but people are used instead of pencil marks! Guests are separated into two equal teams and each team allocates a captain. The captains of each team call out the moves in turn, ordering his players to sit on whichever chair he or she chooses. Members of the two teams need to be easily distinguishable; you could have a boys' team and a girls' team, or get all members of one team to wear silly hats. After each game a new captain is chosen for each team.

Winning
The winners are the first team to complete a line of three team members according to the rules of noughts and crosses.

Examples of winning noughts-and-crosses positions

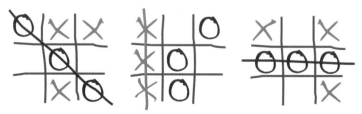

BLIND MAN'S TREASURE HUNT

This is a game for any number of players aged 10 or over. It lasts 5–15 minutes.

You will need
Enough parcels of different sizes and shapes to give one to each player. You will also need a blindfold and a sturdy table.

Playing
Guests leave the room while the parcels are being placed on the table. Guest are led back into the room wearing a blindfold, taken to the table and told they may choose a present by touch alone. Presents must not be opened until everyone has chosen.

Winning
All guests 'win' something in this game. The fun is in guessing what the presents are from their shape and sound. It is fun to inject an element of surprise by putting good gifts in small parcels and silly items in larger presents.

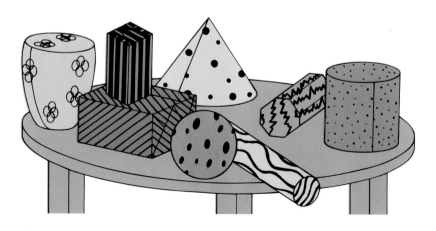

ODD MAN OUT?

This is a game for any number of players aged 10 or over. It lasts 5–15 minutes.

You will need
Enough paper and pencils for all guests.

Preparation
A number of lists are prepared by the host, each containing one item that does not fit with the other items on the list: the odd man out.

Examples of lists and their odd men out (in italics):

1 *New York*, Paris, Tokyo, Rome. (The others are capital cities.)
2 Bee, scorpion, hornet, *flea*. (The others have stings.)
3 Thames, Severn, *Windermere*, Avon. (The others are rivers.)
4 Green, yellow, *pink*, blue. (The others are colours of the rainbow.)
5 Elizabeth, Victoria, Anne, *Belinda*. (The others were British Queens.)
6 Zola, Proust, *Debussy*, Flaubert. (The others were writers.)

Playing
Guests are given a copy of the lists and about ten minutes to write down which item on each list is the odd man out.

Winning
The winner is the player who identifies the most odd men out.

EGG-CUP RACE

This is a game for 2–10 players aged 10 or over. It lasts 5–15 minutes.

You will need
A table-tennis ball and two identical egg-cups for each team. Make sure that the table-tennis ball can be blown out of the egg-cups reasonably easily.

Playing
Divide the guests into two equal teams and have them sit opposite each other at a table. Place two egg-cups in front of the first player from each team and put the table-tennis ball in one of them. The egg cups should be no more than 2 cm (³/₄ in) apart. On the command 'Go!' the first player in each team has to try and blow the ball out of one egg-cup and into the other. Once the first player has managed this, the next team member must try.

Winning

The winning team is the first one in which all team members complete the challenge.

JOIN THE DOTS!

This is a game for any number of players aged 5–10 years. It lasts a minimum of 5 minutes.

You will need
Lots of paper and pencils.

Playing
Players draw seven dots in any arrangement on their piece of paper. It is a good idea if dots are not too close together as this will make the game difficult. When everyone has drawn their dots, all players swap their papers so that nobody has their own paper. A category is then chosen; it could be anything from animals to buildings to vehicles. All players then have five minutes to draw the outline of a picture which incorporates all seven dots on their paper. The picture must be of something in the chosen category.

Winning
The winner should be decided on the basis of how well the players have incorporated the dots into their drawings.

SPOT THE PARENT!

This is a game for 2–10 players aged 10 or over. It lasts as long as you wish.

You will need
A photograph of one parent or guardian of each of the guests, taken when the parents or guardians were children themselves. Ask for these in advance of the party, or ask the guests to bring the photographs with them. You will also need enough sticky labels for all guests, and pencils and paper for all players.

Playing
Pin all the photographs onto a board and number them for easy identification. Ask each player to write their name on a sticky label and attach it to the front of their clothing where it can be seen by other guests. The challenge is for players to try and match the parents or guardians to other players at the party. Keep the photographs on display all the time and get players to guess right at the end of the party.

Winning
The winner is the player with the most correct guesses.

WHERE AM I?

This is a game for 2–10 players aged 10 or over. It lasts a minimum of 15 minutes.

You will need

Enough paper and pencil for all players and about 20 photographs of famous places that have been cut out of magazines and holiday brochures.

Playing

All pictures are numbered and laid out in full view of all players. Everybody has five (or ten) minutes to guess the names of each place or resort. Players should list their answers against the appropriate numbers.

Winning

The winner is the player who correctly identifies the most places.

THE LEANING TOWER

This is a game for any number of players aged 10 or over. It lasts a minimum of 5 minutes. No special equipment is needed.

Playing

Divide the guests into three or more equal teams and get them to stand close together in their team groups. Each team has 10 lives. When the host calls out 'Lean to the front', all players should lean forward as far as possible without moving their feet. Anyone who stumbles or falls over loses a life for their team. Teams must follow any command given, such as 'Lean to the right', or 'Lean backwards', without falling or moving their feet.

Winning

After 10 commands the team with the most lives left is the winner.

THE CATERPILLAR

This is a game for any number of players aged 10 or over. It lasts 5–15 minutes.

You will need
A stopwatch and a chair for each player.

Playing
Arrange the chairs in a circle in the middle of the room. One player stands in the middle of the circle of chairs and the other players sit on chairs in the circle. There should be one spare chair left empty. The seated players are the

'caterpillar' and must move in the same direction from chair to chair in order to prevent the player in the middle of the circle from finding a place. The centre player must try and find a seat without pushing or shoving the other players. All members of the 'caterpillar' must move in the same direction, either clockwise or anticlockwise. When the centre player does eventually manage to get into a seat the person seated to his left becomes the centre player.

Winning
This game is played for fun only – there is no winner!

GOING AWAY?

This is a game for 2–10 players aged 5 or over. It lasts 5–15 minutes.

You will need
A selection of old clothes packed into two suitcases, one for female clothes and one for male clothes.

Playing

Guests are divided into two equal teams, a boys' team and a girls' team. To start, both teams should stand as far as possible from their suitcase. On the command 'GO!' the first player from each team hops to his or her team's suitcase, opens it and puts on some of the clothes, wigs or anything else that is inside. They then pick up their suitcase and hop back to the starting line where they remove the clothes and put them back inside. The same player then hops back with the full case, drops it, and runs to the start line. The next team member in line then performs the same routine.

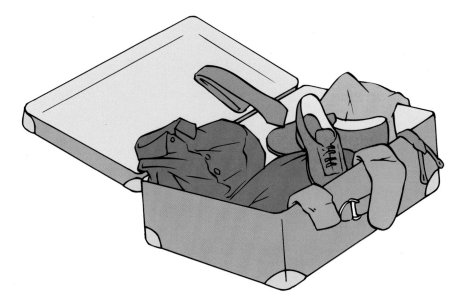

Winning

The winners are the first team in which every team member completes these actions.

AUDITIONS

This is a game for 2–10 players aged 10 or over. It lasts 5–15 minutes.

You will need
Enough paper and pencils for all players.

Preparation
Prepare a list of popular films along with the name of the main female star in each one.

Examples of some films and their leading ladies:

Breakfast at Tiffany's (AUDREY HEPBURN)

Cabaret (LIZA MINELLI)

Casablanca (INGRID BERGMAN)

Ghost (DEMI MOORE)

Mary Poppins (JULIE ANDREWS)

Silence of the Lambs (JODIE FOSTER)

Some Like it Hot (MARILYN MONROE)

Star Wars (CARRIE FISHER)

The Prime of Miss Jean Brodie (MAGGIE SMITH)

Playing
Read out the title of each film in turn. Players must try to write down its leading lady.

Winning
The winner is the player who correctly identifies the most leading ladies.